John George Butler

The Luther statue at the National capital

History--unveiling--addresses

John George Butler

The Luther statue at the National capital
History--unveiling--addresses

ISBN/EAN: 9783337126933

Printed in Europe, USA, Canada, Australia, Japan

Cover: Foto ©ninafisch / pixelio.de

More available books at **www.hansebooks.com**

H.H.Nachulz. Sc.

THE

LUTHER STATUE

AT THE

NATIONAL CAPITAL.

HISTORY—UNVEILING—ADDRESSES.

EDITED BY

J. G. BUTLER.

Pastor Luther Place Memorial Church.

· · ◆ · ·

WASHINGTON, D. C.
GIBSON BROS., PRINTERS, 525 SEVENTH STREET
1886

CONTENTS

DEDICATED

TO THE FRIENDS OF CONSTITUTIONAL LIBERTY

IN THE UNITED STATES OF AMERICA,

THE REPUBLIC WHOSE VITAL PRINCIPLE

WAS ASSERTED BY MARTIN LUTHER AT WORMS.

"HIER STEHE ICH."

Luther Statue Association.

Incorporated by Congress.

J. G. MORRIS, D. D., LL. D.,
President.

G. A. DOBLER,
Recording Secretary

CHARLES A. SCHIEREN,
Treasurer.

J. G. BUTLER,
Corresponding Secretary.

A. J. D. WEDEMEYER,
J. W. B. DOBLER,
AUGUSTUS KOUNTZE,
GEORGE RYNEAL, Jr.,
DANIEL M. FOX.

Luther and the Statue.

By the Editor.

The unveiling of a statue of Martin Luther, the first in the United States, and in the Nation's Capital, marks an epoch in the history of Protestantism.

It is fitting that this first statue of the Reformer should stand among the monuments that beautify the Capital of our Republic, a republic which, under God, but for Luther, had not been. Michelet, the Catholic historian of France, calls Luther "the restorer of liberty in modern times, the liberator of modern thought." Our own Webster says "the assertion and maintenance of religious liberty have their source in the Reformation of Luther, and this love of religious liberty brings with it an ardent devotion to the principles of civil liberty."

The foundations of our Republic lie back of the Declaration of Independence, even beyond Plymouth Rock and the Mayflower; they were laid by the granite, Alpine man of faith and of courage at Erfurt and Wittenberg and Worms. When Columbus discovered this Western world and dedicated it to Christ, Luther was a boy at Eisleben. He was born in 1483. The four hundredth anniversary of his birth stirred all Christendom as it has never been stirred by the birth of any man. Since Paul no man like him has lived.

Luther stands in the world's heart for free thought, free men, free Government, whose Magna Charta is the Bible. This liberated his own conscience from all enslavement, and was ever the focal power of his life and of his work. The Reformation, in which this emancipated monk was the central figure, was both radical and conservative. With all the energy of his honest, earnest soul he hurled Heaven's enginery against the usurpations of a corrupt hierarchy. His ultimate appeal ever was to the Word of God. With equal earnestness he contended for the freedom of every individual, for the right of private judgment, your God given and inalienable inheritance and mine. Our own honored Bancroft says, truly, " Luther repelled the use of violence in religion ; he protested against propagating reform by persecution, and, with a wise moderation, he maintained the sublime doctrine of freedom of conscience."

The church bearing Luther's name and circling the world with his faith, preaching the gospel in most of the languages of Christendom, and numbering fifty millions of people in its communion, has always been marked by its Scriptural conservatism. If there be found within its fold those who are intolerant and exclusive, there is nothing in the life or spirit of the Reformer to warrant any such intolerance. The spirit of sect is wholly in conflict with the gospel ; " In essentials unity, in non-essentials liberty, in all things charity." It was not his friends, but his enemies, who, in derision, called his followers Lutherans. He would be known only as a defender of the gospel, hence the historic name, Evangelical Lutheran Church.

The conserving power of our growing Republic, representing so many and diverse nationalities, is this same Bible with which the Reformer fought the battles of the sixteenth century. Great perils environ us. We are young among the nations, the history

of whose rise and fall suggests both our danger and our duty.
The agitating and unsolved problems of to-day, the problems
that center in our immense immigration, in Socialism, in Mor-
monism, in the liquor power, in our rapidly growing wealth,
and in the unrest of labor, can find their solution alone in the
well defined principles of truth and purity and justice and
equity of the Word of God. Jehovah is the supreme law giver
and final arbiter. Through Moses and the Christ have we the
underlying principles and framework of all abiding government. "As ye would that men should do to you do ye even
so to them," is the germ principle, the seed corn of eternal
right between man and man. "The nation and kingdom
that will not serve God will perish ; yea, those nations shall be
utterly wasted," is the suggestive fiat of prophecy, confirmed
and illustrated in the history of the world's governments.

All lovers of constitutional freedom revere the memory of
Luther. He stands a Gibraltar, defying the wild surgings of
tyranny, whether civil or religious. Despotism and anarchy
alike fall before the spirit of the man who champions the freedom wherewith Christ makes free. The sceptre of His kingdom is a sceptre of righteousness, and that alone will survive
the wreck of nations.

It is fitting, too, that this statue, so full of inspiration, should
adorn the picturesque Memorial Church, itself standing among
the monuments of the Capital a memorial of God's goodness
in delivering our land from bondage and from war, a memorial
of freedom and of peace—a freedom and peace secured and
perpetuated alike to every citizen of the Republic by the Word
of God. Our land has had its days of darkness and its baptism of blood. In the darkest days of the Reformation, which
also had its martyrs, Luther was wont to say to his bosom

friend, Melancthon, "Come, Philip, let us sing." The 46th Psalm became the battle song of the Reformers, and is classic.

"A mighty fortress is our God,
A bulwark never failing.
*   *   *   *   *
And though the world with devils filled
Should threaten to undo us,
We will not fear for God hath willed
His truth to triumph through us."

Jehovah, the God of our fathers, is "*our* refuge and strength, a very present help in trouble; therefore, will not we fear."

" Protect us by Thy might,
Great God, our King."

The Feast of Unveiling.

Flowers and plants abundant and rare, from the Goverment and private conservatories; "Jesus" in gas jets, with a large oil painting of Luther beneath, made the Memorial Church fragrant and beautiful during the joyous Feast of Unveiling.

A fitting prelude was the gathering of the Lutheran Sunday schools of the city on the afternoon of the Lord's day preceding. The services of song, interspersed with prayer, and, the Word, with addresses, made a spirited convocation.

At night the Rev. Dr. F. W. Conrad gave to a large audience his masterly oration upon Luther, the Reformer.

Tuesday evening a platform meeting, in the Memorial, was full of enthusiasm. Gen. James A. Ekin, U. S. A., one of the helpful friends of the Statue movement, was announced to preside. Stirring addresses were made by the Rev. Drs. Jacob Fry, D. H. Geissinger, D. M. Gilbert, Joel Swartz and Hon. Jacob F. Miller.

Rev. Dr. M. Sheeleigh read a poem.

Poem by Rev. Dr. M. Sheeleigh.

Lift up the gladsome voice!
Let millions now rejoice
Responsive to our cheer,
As, met for high commemoration,
We join, in sight of every nation,
With reverent praisefulness a "Stone of Help" to rear!

Four hundred years have run
Their course beneath the sun
Since, far beyond the sea,
A man of giant soul was given,
To work a wonder-work for Heaven;
And hence with joyful hearts we mark this jubilee.

How fitting that to-day
The eager throngs should pay
Such tribute loved and true!—
That in this Nation's Capital
Erect doth stand, and ever shall,
This mould of manliness each age will hail anew!

There let it ever stand,
That form which Art hath planned,
That semblance wrought in bronze;
Though mute, and destitute of motion.
Around it men shall bring devotion—
Devotion to their God, and honor to His sons.

When Heav'n of human hands
Some special work demands,
His prescience hath prepared
A Moses, Daniel, or a Paul,
Or LUTHER, for the mighty call
That breaks th' eventful day when His own arm is bared.

A night all dark and dread
Had far and farther spread,
Through age on age, deep wrong;
For truth, prevailed the plagues of error,
The Church of Christ was rent in terror,—
And many, groaning, cried, "How long, O Lord, how long?"

Behold one—born of race
That scorns to fear the face
Of strongest, direst foeman;
That ne'er would basely stoop or cower
In presence of an earthly power—
Though holding modern fort or wall of ancient Roman.

Not rocked on courtly knees,
Nor clad in robes of ease,
'Mid enervating things;
But forced to ways of self-denial,
And disciplined in rugged trial,
The Lord His servant forth to painful toiling brings.

By grace of Heav'n renewed,
With martyr-faith imbued,
Filled with consuming zeal,
Of hero-souls set in the van,
God brings this marvel of a man
The pow'rs for ill allied to brave for human weal.

That statue's antitype,
For his high calling ripe,
Through God the giant foiled;
Before the haughty and the vaunting
Striking for truth, with soul undaunting,
Till startled pope and kings beneath their crowns recoiled.

The might that in him wrought,
With grace from heaven fraught
For all the lands abroad,
The hero-life within him nursed,
Which forth in grand achievement burst,
And toned "Ein' Feste Burg" with glory to our God.

Give praises to the Lord,
For gospel truth restored,
And echoed far and wide
To all the waiting nations rung
By His anointed servant's tongue—
That we by living faith in Christ are justified.

Where'er the truth o'er earth
Most freely marches forth,
And souls doth liberate,—
There breathes, with healthful demonstration—
There pulsates *now* the Reformation—
Thence myriad tongues in this your joy participate.

Though throngs, who press the ground,
This artist-pile around,
Fresh inspiration find,
Long hath his monument been known
To rest on firmer base than stone—
Ev'n in the deathless hearts of rising human-kind.

Had *ears* of man ne'er heard
The world-resounding word
That tells of Luther born,
Our *eyes* could not have looked upon
That stately shaft to Washington,
Which seeks the skies and greets the earliest beams of morn.

And had the world ne'er heard,
The words that in him stirred,
And plead for liberty,
Those walls, dome-crowned against the sky,
Should not have gladdened human eye,
Type of a people's power whom God hath spoken free.

From his day comes there still
The liberating thrill,
With voice of heavenly call,—
As Truth from tyranny delivers—
Inner and outer bondage shivers,
Though earth and hell combine to hold mankind in thrall.

And yet, for future time
Wait triumphs more sublime,
When men, the nations o'er,
In signs of joy-proclaiming light,
Will semaphore, from height to height,
The gospel victories on every mundane shore.

Long as with earnest heart
That cherished work of Art
By countless eyes is viewed,
They'll read what *faith* is pictured there,
What wondrous potency of *pray'r*,
What *prophet-life and fire* in look and attitude.

There, firm on granite base,
With Heav'n imploring face,
That symbol stand through time;
To speak, adown the lapsing ages,
What History traced upon her pages
To thrill with joyfulness the men of every clime.

" Stand! that colossal form,
Facing the rushing storm
Unmoved as 'neath the light;
As Luther faced careering wrath
Which o'er him fain would plough its path—
But which in weakness broke before Jehovah's might.

There let it *ever* be
A sign of thought set free,
Of unbound tongue and will,
Of shackles from the conscience riven,
Of wider field to learning given,
And of God's Book unsealed—all men with joy to fill.

There let that image stand,
The while the clenchéd hand
Is on the Bible pressed,
In token of the soul's appealing
From man's device to God's revealing,
Of Truth the one—the sure—the everlasting test.

There let it stand for aye—
Long as the orb of day
And nightly hosts behold;
There stand, perpetual witness giving—
In praise to God, the Ever-living—
For holy, highest Truth, which doth all hope infold.

Long as that head shall there
Be lifted high in air,
Heedless of malice hurled,
His work, whose fame is there attested,
Shall more and more be manifested,
As God's unfettered Truth emancipates the world.

Thus, while the centuries,
Unresting as the seas,
Roll onward, one by one,
This chosen of the Lord shall still
His mission through the *earth* fulfill,
Standing, to gazing eyes, like Uriel in the sun.

Day of Unveiling.

Heaven never smiled more serenely than upon the 21st of May, the day of the unveiling. Mr. A. J. D. Wedemeyer, of New York, gracefully presided at a morning meeting; the hymns of Luther were sung. The Revs. F. F. Burmeyer and Albert Hounrighaus conducted the devotional exercises, and the Rev. Drs. F. Ph. Hennighausen, A. C. Wedekind and E. Moldehnke, made addresses of great power in the German language.

It is estimated that from 7,000 to 10,000 people witnessed the ceremonies around the Statue. The pulpit of Washington was largely represented upon the platform. The Martin Luther Society, of New York City, together with large delegations from Philadelphia, Baltimore, Harrisburg, York, Lancaster, Gettysburg, Hagerstown, Frederick, Winchester and Richmond, besides representatives from distant parts of the country, extending even beyond the Missouri River, were present. The General Assembly of the Presbyterian Church, in session at Saratoga, N. Y., and which had been invited to attend the unveiling, wired its congratulations and regrets through the Rev. Dr. Geo. P. Hayes, Moderator. The names of the many Lutheran pastors present, other than those who filled places in the programme, would add interest to the narrative, but it was not possible to secure a complete list. Very many of them evinced the liveliest interest in the Statue

movement from its inception to the unveiling. Largely
through their activity, seconded by the liberality of the laity,
was it made possible for the Statue Association to announce
all bills paid, and a small surplus in the Treasury, safely in-
vested, for incidentals that may arise in the future care of the
Statue and grounds. The press of Washington, always full
of enterprise, rendered valuable services to the Luther Statue
Association, and, in connection with the Unveiling, published
cuts of the Colossal Bronze with full reports of the proceedings.
Mr. Justice Miller, of the Supreme Court of the United States,
presided; the Rev. Dr. F. W. Conrad and the Rev. Bishop A.
D. Payne were the Chaplains.

History of the Statue.

Prepared by order of the Luther Statue Association.

For several years earnest friends of Luther and of his great work had agitated the planting of a statue of the German Reformer in our country, but by reason of insuperable difficulties, chiefly with reference to location, had not been able to accomplish the grand work.

To Mr. Charles A. Schieren, of New York City, belongs the honor of having first suggested the idea of a statue of Luther upon the fine site in front of the Memorial Church, to be known hereafter as "Luther Place." The Washington correspondent of the LUTHERAN OBSERVER, "B," in one of his letters, spoke of the suggestion of Mr. Schieren. Dr. J. G. Morris, of Baltimore, another correspondent of the OBSERVER, always fired by the mention of Luther, seconded, with his racy pen, that suggestion.

Falling under the eye of Mr. G. A. Dobler, of Baltimore, he at once entered into correspondence with the Pastor of the Memorial Church, sending photographs of the Worms Luther and a copy of correspondence which he had already had with Lauchhammer, at whose renowned foundries the original bronze had been cast. Mr. Dobler suggested the names of Mr. A. J. D. Wedemeyer and Mr. J. W. B. Dobler, of New York City, with whom correspondence was at once opened.

In reply to a letter to Mr. Augustus Kountze, of New York, a prompt and liberal subscription came, as did also a cheerful response from Mr. George Ryneal, Jr., of Washington, D. C. These gentlemen, with the addition of Hon. Daniel M. Fox, of Philadelphia, suggested by the editor of the OBSERVER, formed themselves into an association for the accomplishment of the object whose consummation calls together this multitude of people to-day in the National Capital from all parts of our common country.

February 14, 1883, a circular was issued asking for funds, and designating the banking houses of Kountze Brothers, of New York City, J. A. H. Becker, of Baltimore, and M. D. Harter, of Mansfield, Ohio, all of whom were helpful to the work, as depositories.

The papers of the Lutheran Church generally gave the subject an endorsement, some more, some less hearty. "Luther Statue Notes" appeared weekly in the columns of the OBSERVER from its Washington correspondent. The religious press of the country generally endorsed and commended the project, whilst the secular press freely published all items furnished it. Some diversion from the main purpose of the Association was occasioned by the question of *location*, raised chiefly in Washington, the hope being expressed that permission might be had to put our Luther upon one of the public reservations. This, however, was soon found to be utterly impracticable as well as unnecessary.

So prompt and hearty, from city and hamlet, were the responses to the appeal of the circular that the Association unanimously felt warranted in ordering the statue by cablegram on the 12th of April, less than two months from the date of the circular. The hope then was that it might be ready for unveiling by the 10th of November, the four hundredth

anniversary of the Reformer's birth, an event whose observ-
ance was general and hearty throughout the Christian world.

It was soon learned, however, that the statue could not be
secured at so early a date. In the meanwhile, the Memorial Evangelical Lutheran Church, at a congregational meeting, authorized its trustees to transfer to the Statue Association, so soon as incorporated, so much of the triangle south of
the church as was needed for the location of this magnificent
bronze.

The members of the Memorial Church evinced the most
generous interest in the Luther Monument. The Feast of
Unveiling culminated in a bounteous collation in the Chapel,
provided by the ladies, which was enlivened by impromptu
addresses, for visiting friends.

Two meetings of the Statue Association were held in Philadelphia and one in Washington, at which last meeting pre-
liminary steps were taken looking toward the unveiling. The
completed programme, arranged by correspondence, is here-
with incorporated, and a copy has been deposited in the
pedestal.

The Association placed in the pedestal, a copper box, her-
metically sealed, containing—

1. A copy of the Word of God.
2. A copy of Köstlin's Life of Luther.
3. A copy of Luther's Smaller Catechism.
4. A copy of Stalls' Lutheran Year Book.
5. A copy of the Lutheran Almanac for 1884.
6. A United States Blue Book.
7. Copies of the papers published by the Lutheran Church,
   and of the City of Washington.
8. A history of the Association, and a list of contributors to
   the Luther Statue Fund.

It is worthy of mention that the North German Lloyd Steamship Company transported, free, from Hamburg to Baltimore, this Statue; that the Baltimore & Ohio Railroad Company rendered similar service from Baltimore to Washington, and that the Messrs. Sprigmann & Brother, of this city, generously tendered similar service from the depot to the "Luther Place." On account of unforseen difficulties, but for the timely and generous co-operation of the Hon. Secretary of War, Robert T. Lincoln, Col. Thos. L. Casey, U. S. Engineers, in charge of the State, War and Navy building and of the Washington Monument, and the Hon. Omar D. Conger, U. S. Senator from Michigan, this Statue would not be unveiled to-day. The thanks of the Luther Statue Association and its friends are hereby tendered.

The Statue Association, in the presence of this immense concourse of people, of every nationality and of every creed, but entering into a common joy, render devout thanks to Almighty God, who has given His blessing to this their humble endeavor to advance the cause of Truth and Righteousness.

A Justice of the Supreme Court of the United States dignifies the occasion by presiding at this meeting, whilst an honored Senator of the United States, O. D. Conger, of the State of Michigan, joins the venerable President of our Association in fitting words of eulogy in memory of Luther, whose name and fame are more enduring than this colossal bronze.

As the veil shall uncover the Statue, Luther's battle hymn, the now classic "*Ein Feste Burg*," by the United States Marine Band, will tell of the abiding faith and courage of the man whom God has honored, the great Protestant, whose name becomes more lasting as the ages roll on.

By order of the Luther Statue Association:

J. G. BUTLER,
Corresponding Secretary.

Hon. O. D. Conger's Address.

The Hon. O. D. Conger, LL. D., Senator of the United States, from Michigan, being introduced, said:

MR. PRESIDENT: We stand in the presence of the veiled Statue of one who dwelt upon the earth four hundred years ago, whose influence and honors have spread from the hamlet of his nativity, in the heart of Germany, adown the waters of time in ever widening circles until they have encompassed the world.

Four centuries from the date of his birth, three thousand miles from the scenes of his labor, on the borders of a continent then undiscovered, in the Capital of a wonderful Nation then unborn, we gather from far and near around the Monument of Martin Luther, wrought in enduring bronze from the mines of Germany, moulded by the skillful artisans of his own Fatherland, and transported over intervening land and sea to stand amidst the other memorials of patriotism and veneration that adorn our beautiful city, and stimulate the faith and virtue of unnumbered citizens of this commonwealth.

Justice Miller, of the Supreme Court, presides over the ceremonies. Senators and representatives in Congress bring the homage of respect from multitudes of people from their several States. Ministers of all creeds, and Christians of a common faith, and all who desire the regeneration and exaltation of the human race, who demand complete toleration of religious belief, who trust in the limitless expansion of intellectual vigor, who hope for perpetual growth of freedom and faith in the soul, are assembled here to render their tribute of respect to the memory of the great Reformer, and to dedicate his enduring Monument in the court of this Lutheran Memorial Church on the border of a circle already adorned with a splendid statue of one of our most illustrious soldier heroes.

Mr. President, surrounded by such scenes, thrilled by such memories, subdued by the mysterious influence of such a life and character, the proudest and most self-reliant of us all must leave unanswered the perpetually recurring inquiry—What has he done, this peasant boy of Eisleben, this sweet singer of Eisenach, this young Augustinian monk of Erfurt, this secluded prisoner of Wartburg, this professor in the University of Wittenburg, this Reformer of Germany, this loved and venerated apostle of Christendom? Indeed, what great things must he not have done to have won and worn the high esteem, the ardent affection, the more than imperial honors, and world-wide renown that crowned him in life, and enshrined his memory in the hearts of succeeding generations so long as time endures.

In the brief time allotted to me I will not even outline his life and character and works, nor is there any necessity, did time and ability permit.

On the 10th day of November, 1883, the four hundredth anniversary of Luther's birthday, and in the near time thereof, from pulpit and rostrum and press in every Christian community on the globe, sermons, addresses, memorials, biographies and histories of the life and times of this great man were poured forth with such superfluity of abundance that to renew them in almost any form would suggest plagiarism in the discourse, and unwarranted ignorance in the audience.

While, therefore, I shall leave to others, better fitted by their duty and profession, the interesting labor of presenting the religious and theological questions involved in the discussions of those soul stirring controversies and spiritual conflicts which

shook the world and changed the doctrine of nations and em-
pires, and gave such mighty impulses to the onward and up-
ward progress of our race, I may be permitted to allude to
some episodes in the life of our hero, to some influences about
that time arousing the world from the slumber and lethargy
of the dark ages, and to some of the consequences of that
spiritual and intellectual awakening of which Germany was the
battle ground and Martin Luther the central figure of strength.

In imagination we may revisit the scenes of his life, and sur-
round ourselves with the imagery of the land and the people
where he dwelt.   You will see the dark Thuringian forest of
Saxony, its gloomy woods of fir and pine, with mysterious
voices forever sounding through its leafy aisles, the wild
huntsman dashing along its mountain crests, the spectral rider
sounding his horn in pursuit of the deer.

> By midnight moons,
> O'er moistening dews,
> In vestments of the chase arrayed,
> The hunter still
> The deer pursues,
> The hunter and the deer a shade.

In the gorges of the mountains are dark mines and caverns
filled with all imaginable ghosts and goblins guarding the
treasures of the earth and the gems of the mine, all real and
terrible to that peasant boy of Eisleben as well as to all the
dwellers in that mysterious region.   What marvel that his
mind was filled with images of demons to fight and with personal devils to encounter?   What marvel that he would crush
one devil with his ink stand, and would go to the supreme
trial at Worms, though he believed the devils were as thick as
tiles on the houses?   In God's name he would go on.

In the villages and gardens of the beautiful valleys were

fruits and flowers, and singing birds, and laughing children, and rural sports, and bands of singing youths, then, as now, the children of music and of song.

What marvel that Luther's heart was full of music and his voice of song ; that he wrote hymns and songs and set them to music through all his life, hymns and songs and music that have flashed with electric speed from throbbing human hearts to the ear of One who is forever touched with our infirmities, and who hath borne the infinite sorrows of our race ?

In all that German land were the pure, cheerful Saxon homes, the loving Teutonic families, the virtuous matron and maid. What marvel, then, that the priest, when casting aside the doctrine of papal supremacy and the Romish ritual, should likewise reject monkish celibacy and the nun's seclusion, and restore to the ministry the sacred relations of the family, and to the nun the endearing enjoyments of home ?

Having, whether providentially or by chance, had occasional opportunities to study the Latin bible in the monastery at Erfurt, and learned the marvelous treasures which were unrevealed in the German language and almost unknown to the Latin scholar, whether layman or priest, what marvel that his prison in the Castle of Wartburg became the most illustrious " school of the prophets" whence issued from his glowing pen that glorious version of the gospel, not only the word of life but also the perennial fountain of pure German literature which has, more than anything else, preserved alike the faith and the language of the Teutonic races.

These few references must suffice for mere personal incidents and allusions.

There are, aside from the spiritual experiences and religious struggles and triumphs of this stalwart champion of truth, many things in the history of the times in which he lived, and the conditions of the nations of the earth, and the state of human society, and the mental and spiritual awakening which about those days spread over the world, that demand the consideration of those who would comprehend the marvelous changes and progress of the opening years of the sixteenth century. Before that time the art of printing had been invented. More deadly war material came into use. The Turk had driven alike the spiritual and temporal powers of Christendom from Asia and from parts of Europe; the Crescent had triumphed over the Cross in the powerful bishopric of Alexandria, in all Arabia, in all the region of the wonderful cities beyond Jordan, in the Holy Land itself. The minarets of Islam towered above the foundations of the sacred temple, and the Christian crept in abject disguise to weep by night near the place of his Redeemer's supulchre. In Antioch, where they were first named, the Christian was unknown. In all the land of the Seven Churches the religion of Mahomet had absolute sway. The Turk passed the Hellespont, and the Empire of Constantine was blotted out. Greece and Macedon yielded to the false Prophet, and the Moslem cry of the muezzin echoed along the shores of the Danube even to the gates of Vienna. The most beautiful part of Spain had been long the conquest of Moorish Mohammedism. Indeed the Christendom of the early centuries had been driven from Asia and Africa and eastern Europe until its frontier was well nigh beyond the lands of apostolic visitation. While more fiery zeal was kindled in the breasts of the deluded followers of Mahommed, an infinite lethargy benumbed the disciples of the Cross. The church, after spasmodic crusades to redeem the holy sepulchre, slumbered amid its formalities and ceremonials, relinquished vast realms of its former control to wage war upon the faith and conscience of its individual members.

Through all these dark ages, while continents were passing
from its control, and vast domains were wrested from its influence, the church at least retained the only records of our
holy religion, the literature and knowledge of former ages, and
with its Reformation made possible the marvelous progress of
modern times.   As a harbinger of the great Reformation, the
Christian powers drove back the Turk from the walls of Vienna,
adown the Danube and beyond the Balkans.   In Spain, in the
very year that Luther was born, Ferdinand and Isabella com-
menced the eight years' war which drove the Moors from
Spain and reclaimed to Christendom some of its fairest prov-
inces.   And in that self same year Columbus left the Court of
John of Portugal, weary and discouraged with eight years of
promise and denial of aid, for his great voyage of discovery,
and for the next eight years, until 1492, both in court and
camp offered to the sovereigns of Castile and Arragon the sovereignty of a new world.   Before Luther's manhood the Por-
tugese had encompassed Africa; Columbus had discovered
America; wonderful stories of wonderful lands were on every
tongue; unknown oceans were explored, unknown races of
men were found; dreams of wealth and visions of empire,
greed for gold and zeal for conversion, were mingled in strange
confusion in the minds of saint and sinner.   All the world was
aroused; the hope of converting the strange heathen races
quickened spiritual activity.   The same ship bore the explorer
with his sword and the priest with his gospel, to conquer realms
and redeem souls.   The courtier left the palace, the monk his
cell; the cavalier forsook his pleasures and the Puritan his
home, to found colonies and churches in far off lands.   We
have not been told, we may never know, how far the direct or
the mysterious influences of such startling events awaken alike
the moral and intellectual forces of our being; how voice

answereth to voice and deep unto deep, until along the myntic chord of sympathy the heart of humanity is moved by a common impulse to holier aspirations and purer sacrifice.   But we may well believe that the great heart of Luther throbbed with quickened pulsation to the influences which were arousing the world.   That the old Saxon spirit which was then commencing that career of control and supremacy which has already encircled the globe, and will hereafter control its destinies, was then strong in him ; that he was the true representative of those Teutonic forces which are being developed in all the progressive nations, and are the very fountain and source of most of the marvelous inventions and grand discoveries of this most wonderful age.   He walked in the valley of humiliation, and he strode along the high places of power ; he comforted and sustained the lowly in their sorrow, and he thundered anathemas upon the proudest in their sins.   Exhorting unceasingly to all good works, he ever bore upon the folds of his banner the motto and watchword, " The just shall live by Faith." He rebuked with equal vigor the oppression of the nobility and the communism and revenges of the peasantry.   Spiritual pride was, if possible, less offensive to his soul than slavish humility.

Liberty of conscience, personal responsibility of man, an existence of probation on earth, the resurrection of the body and the immortality of the soul.   With such a theme rounding the tragic history of every spirit that emerges unconscious from the unrevealed beginning of existence to tread thenceforth the dark or the luminous pathways of eternity—

> " We feel our immortality o'ersweep
>   All time, all tears, all pain, all fears,
> Pealing, like the eternal thunders of the deep,
>   This truth into our ears.
>   Ye live forever."

Among those great, " those immortal names that were not
born to die," the world of humanity has enthroned Martin
Luther.   Conspicuous in the capital of a nation whose possi-
bility of existence hinged upon his labors in life, and the
adoption of the principles he taught till his death, we this day
place this memorial of our veneration.   May it endure for the
centuries to come an emblem of human progress and immortal hope.   But should the ravages of time corrode and
wear away the enduring bronze and crumble the solid granite,
may this Capital of our glorious commonwealth still remain
the living heart and center of a Nation of united freemen,
more happy than our imagination can picture, advanced in all
the elements of goodness and greatness beyond our fondest
dreams, blessing and blessed by the untold millions who shall
enter into our glorious inheritance and perpetuate the sublime
institutions established by our fathers and preserved by the
infinite Ruler of the Universe.

Rev. J. G. Morris' Address.

The Rev. J. G. Morris, D. D., LL. D., President of the Luther Statue Association, followed Senator Conger, and said:
All hail! my fellow believers present, as well as the whole
Protestant community of our land, upon the auspicious event
which has brought so many of us together this day.   After
many months of labor, anxiety, self-denial and some fruitless opposition, and not a small degree of indifference, we are
happy in beholding the consummation of our ardent wishes
and the successful result of our earnest exertions.

We live to see the completion of a work, which was never
before undertaken in this country—the erection of a statue to

the illustrious Martin Luther. Statesmen, heroes, benefactors, jurists, artists and divines have been honored by our grateful people, but never before has the greatest of them all been thus distinguished. In his own fatherland numerous statues have been erected to his memory, and not less than five or six within the last few years.

It was becoming that we, American admirers of the mighty Reformer, and we especially who ecclesiastically bear his honored name, should follow this bright example and behold before us the realization of our work.

The Protestant Church could not excite such a universal enthusiasm about any other ecclesiastical character since the days of Paul—no, never.

There have been many mighty men before Luther; there were many strong men cotemporary with him, some of whom were his co-laborers, and a few of whom may have been even more learned than he was; but we cannot make a church hero of any of them, though they were great and good men. Luther is the embodiment of the whole of them; head and shoulders above them all, the *colossus* of the gallery, the giant of the group.

Star after star rose in radiant splendor in the dark church heavens, and shed through space their cheerful light; but amid this galaxy of lights, which studded the firmament, Luther shone forth the brightest of them all, whose blazing rays penetrated deeper into the gloom and dispelled it as with a flash.

He was the only man in all the ages at the remembrance of whose inappreciable services the heart of Protestantism bounds with rapture; his name rings like the sound of a silver trumpet through the generations, and the echoes of it will never cease to be heard. Luther is not a sectarian name;

it belongs to the whole Christian Church; all unite in celebrating him as the glorious instrument chosen of God to perform the mighty work; his name and work are now more
frequently mentioned, his writings more frequently quoted,
more books are published about him, and his invaluable services are more highly rated, than ever before.

In nearly every century before, there had been some good
men who wrote and preached against the errors of the church;
but they attacked the bad morals practiced rather than the
unscriptural doctrines then believed; and even against these
there was no bold, decided, continued protestation, no chal-
lenge of the theologians to discussion, no extended exposure
of their false teachings.

God brought out Luther, who was himself a monk and
priest; he discerned the errors of the church in faith and practice; his righteous soul was fired with a holy ardor; like
another Elijah, he thundered the truth into the ears of princes
and kings and prelates; like another John Baptist, he proclaimed the coming of the Son of Man in the restoration of
pure doctrine and holy living; he pointed to Christ and said:
"Behold the lamb, instead of your images, pilgrimages,
rosaries, confessions and fastings." He disinterred the gospel
buried in the foul grave of papal sin and gloom.

The mightiest revolution of modern times was the conse-
quence; there was the introduction of new modes of thought
and action; the world seemed to awake as out of a dream;
the truth triumphed and the gospel became free.

The particular occasion was, as you know, the ninety-five
propositions, a story familiar to every intelligent person.

This open defiance in publishing these propositions was only
proclaimed by Luther after all attempts to move the heads of
the church were fruitless. Pope, cardinals and bishops were

called on to reform acknowledged errors and corruptions; they promised, but they failed. Then it was that Luther rose; these propositions were carried into all directions, and created an extraordinary sensation, the attention of multitudes roused new ideas ; new methods of thinking, new ways of doing things were introduced ; there was a resurrection of mind; no new, I mean *original*, faith was preached. It was the *old* faith of the apostles, but reintroduced. It was restored to life, though it was not dead, it only slept. It was brought out fresh from the rubbish which had been allowed to gather upon it for a thousand years ; it was newly cleansed from human additions and abuses. Our Protestant Christianity is not a new religion, but the *old*, like a grand marble monument, showing its original purity after the gathered dust of ages and the gaudy decorations of a vitiated taste have been washed away.

This is the old, fresh, life inspiring, mind enlightening, soul saving gospel taught by the apostles, sanctioned and accepted by the pious of all ages, the light of which had been obscure for centuries. It was hidden under a bushel, and Luther lifted it off; it was concealed behind a curtain, but he drew the curtain aside, and showed the light in all its burning splendor.

Science was extinguished, literature pined in monastic cells, and the bible was mildewed under scholastic rubbish ; the altar was overloaded with meretricious ornaments ; the sacraments were desecrated by unscriptural additions ; the priesthood was the slavish horde of the tyrannical usurper of God's throne, and the people were ignorant, superstitious and degraded ; the gospel was obscured by human inventions, and the world was sunk in the depths of error and sin. The solitary monk who shook the world arose, and liberty and light were restored to the suffering nations.

The church was rescued from the slavery of human authority in religion, from confidence in man for salvation, and from the blighted errors of a false worship.

The bible is the religion of Protestants; the bible alone is our guide. It was this bible which gave liberty to Luther, and it was Luther, with this bible in his hand, who gave liberty to the world. Yes, liberty from a bondage ten fold more galling than chains of tempered iron.

By this touchstone we try the spirits. This is the priceless jewel of gospel liberty in which we rejoice. Look at the difference between us and the Romanist in this respect:

He is bound to believe what the church prescribes, without examination.

We examine and then believe.

He takes everything on credit that is taught without any reflection.

We require proof from the scripture.

He believes what the church teaches.

We believe what the bible teaches.

He never calls into question what he is taught.

We say, even to our minister, you must prove what you teach from the word of God.

He exercises no judgment in such matters.

We exercise private judgment.

This is our Christian liberty.

We do not trust for salvation in human meditations; we, as members of Christ's body, stand in immediate connection with Him; we, as branches, are immediately joined with Christ, the *true vine*. There are no created mediators between Him and us. "One mediator between God and man, the man Christ Jesus." We reject the intercession of the Virgin Mary and the saints, though we may revere them. We do not ask for their help because we do not need it.

Here is our great advantage ; one Lord, one glorious head
" No other name given under heaven whereby we are saved."

Oh, how unlike the cumbrous works of man is the plan of
heaven, so artless, easy and unencumbered. There are no
meretricious arts to beguile us, no clustering ornaments to
clog us. Heaven's plan is as free from ostentation as it is
from weakness. It stands like a glorious rainbow, majestic in
its own simplicity, above the portal of our Protestant Church,
legible by the light thrown upon it by the star of Bethlehem,
stands the soul quickening inscription, " Believe and live."

The Reformation was not a human work; though God em-
ployed human agency; it was a divine work. All the prelim-
inaries showed a direct divine agency; the revival of learning
in Europe; the study of ancient languages; the discovery of
America and of printing ; the growing inquiry among men ; a
sense of their wrongs and oppressions; the spread of light and
the death of martyrs—all these were preparatives directed by
Providence. The world was in a ferment, just as at the time
of the coming of Christ, people were looking for some great
change ; they did not know what it would be. But the times
were exciting ; the church was corrupt in doctrine and morals ;
truth was obscured ; the necessity of a reform was conceded.
At length Luther rose. God endowed him with singular
gifts: unshaken fortitude; dauntless courage; indefatigable
industry; burning zeal; devoted piety; great learning. Such
was the man. He raised him up and protected him; shielded
him amid many dangers; rescued him almost miraculously
out of the hands of the enemy; strengthened him in all bold
enterprises; enabled him to translate the bible and write many
other good books. Thus the work was carried on until hundreds of thousands were converted, and from that day to this
the glorious gospel has had full course.

He stood in the vanguard of the great battle, a genuine
hero, if ever mortal man was heroic.   His character was built
upon a broad foundation of true manhood, and he was a
champion of humanity.   His massive intelligence and saga-
city ; his intellectual courage ; his sincerity ; his simplicity of
life ; his deep tenderness ; his fiery and aggressive energy ; his
keen insight into shams, and his sure grasp of realities ; his
fervent piety ; these were the outlines of a colossal character,
to whom admiring Europe looked as a leader and deliverer.

The time was ripe for such a revolution ; had there been no
Luther the reformation might have come in some form or
other, but it would not have been what it was, and the chances
are that it would not have been so good.

It was Luther's humanity that made Protestantism the religion of the household, as Romanism had been the religion
of the State and of the cathedral.

How shall we honor the memory of this man who, next to
St. Paul, has been the most powerful personality that Christianity has produced ?   It is not by erecting monuments to
him, nor holding conventions ; but, better than these, by the
study of his life and work.   It is not enough to consider a few
of the many striking epochs of his life ; these, wonderful as
they were, were not the real battles of the Reformation.   It is
a good study, this era of the Reformation, and if we could suc-
ceed in leading our churches to pursue it at this anniversary,
it would be well.   For it was a time when men, repudiating
the papal authority, set themselves to the study of the bible as
it had never been studied before.   They sought in the bible
that infallible guide which church authority no longer offered
to the satisfaction of their consciences.   The bible was their
chart, their beacon, their sure stronghold.   It is good to recall such days and to follow such examples.

The Reformation emancipated the enslaved church from
satanic thraldom; the colossal fortress of popery trembled
from summit to foundation from the rude shock it sustained;
the great Luther, with his Bohemian goose quill, pierced
through the mighty fabric and exposed its internal corruptions to an astonished world. By it the baptismal font of
God's house was purified of all idolatry, and the simple though
significative New Testament baptism was reintroduced. On
that day, the apostolic practice of private confession was rescued from all oppression of the conscience, from enforced bodily
mortification, from slavish submission to ecclesiastical tyranny,
from the imposition of unnatural penalties, and groundless
threats of purgatory and damnation. On that day the altar
was purified from the abominations of the mass, and the gospel sacrament of the body and blood of our Lord was rein-
stated. On that day the pulpit was brought back to its
legitimate purpose, and ceased to be the platform for the sale
of indulgences and the publication of fables and falsehoods.
On that day the ministry was elevated to its original dignity
and office of preaching the simple gospel of our Lord, and
laid aside its presumptive arrogance, its greedy avarice, and
its unwarranted claims in hearing auricular confession and
shriving professed penitents. On that day human government received its regeneration, in being emancipated from the
tyranny of Rome, which claimed authority over and above all
human reigning powers and subjects alike. On that day all
poor sinners were taught that they should not seek for com-
fort by invoking the saints, but by trusting only in the merits
of Christ. The dying had reason to rejoice in that day, f r
they were no longer tortured by the apprehensions of purgatory, but if dying in the faith, they would at once be admitted
into heaven. In a word, the universal believing church in one

united voice can exclaim : This is the day the Lord has made ;
we will rejoice and be glad in it; and this is the feeling in
which we all partake.

Our Luther statue to be unveiled to-day has been favorably
noticed by hundreds of secular and religious papers ; the project has been sanctioned, and has secured the approbation and
sympathy of thousands in and out of our church. It will at-
tract still further attention, and for ages to come visitors to the
Capital will gaze with admiration upon the features of that
glorious Reformation hero, while they call to remembrance the
mighty work which Providence selected him to perform.

We expect that many Lutheran nationalities will be there
to participate in the joyous jubilee. Just as the veil falls there
will be one grand swelling, overwhelming burst of happy
song, " Ein feste Burg ist unser Gott ! "

Some may ask us to-day What went ye out to see ? and we
will answer : Not a reed shaken by the wind, but a mighty
oak, as Herder says. The storm rages at the summit, but
thou, O, Luther ! with thy hundred branching arms, standest
fast, and still art green ; not a man in soft raiment and of weak
mind, but a man of brass, solid, firm, unshaken, " even if the
world were full of devils." We have come to see an undaunted
witness of the truth, the unterrified hero. As a man of rock,
he stood unalarmed before princes and potentates ; as an un-
compromising witness, he gave the plain, homely answer, " I
cannot do otherwise." We have come out to see Luther in
imperishable bronze, not sitting behind his desk covered with
books, but standing upon his feet ; not with downcast looks,
but with elevated head, his severe brow challenging storm and
hail, and smiling even at the terrific thunder as it rolls by him,
and at the weird, burning lightning as it plays round his head,
as though he would say, " Here I stand." We come out to see

a pious servant of God, not one of those modern heroes of liberty, who would emancipate us from the obligations of human and divine government; not a besieger of heaven, who would tear the crown from the Almighty; not a church revolutionist, who would overturn the deep foundation of divine truth, but a church Reformer and a restorer of apostolic Christianity.

We come out to see a man standing with the bible in his hand, which he clasps closely to his heart, as though he would say, "God help me." We come out to see the man of prayer; the man who gave God's word to the people in their own language; who restored the true worship; who re-erected the broken-down pulpit. This Luther, with the bible in his hand, seems to exclaim, "I am not ashamed; hear all ye people, the word which I have restored to you, for you will find no substitute for it in the writings of the philosophers, with all their wisdom; nor in your poets, with all their harmonious verse; nor in your discoverers, with all their useful inventions; nor in your statesmen, with all their diplomacy; for other foundation can no man lay than that which is laid, even Christ."

But how are we to account for the universal excitement in the Protestant world on this subject *at this time?* What has lately happened to call the attention of so many hundred thousands to it?

Is Protestantism in peril? No; it never stood firmer.

"How can that be a failure," says a distinguished Presbyterian divine, "which did not exist before 1500, and in 1884 controls 488,000,000 of people, while its rivals, including both the Roman and Greek churches, control only about 280,000,000?"

Is Protestantism declining, requiring a spasmodic effort on the part of its friends to support the shaking fabric? No! It is more powerful and influential than ever; its lukewarm

friends are everywhere awaking to active life; its ardent advo-
cates are renewing their energies; their numbers are increas-
ing; their zeal is growing; its peaceful conquests are rapidly
extending; its weapons are multiplying, for more than a mil-
lion of bibles are printed and circulated every year; its presses
are publishing the most substantial religious literature; its
pulpits are everywhere proclaiming salvation by faith in the
Son of God; its Sunday schools are teaching the gospel to
five millions of children; its missionaries are bearing the light
of life to the heathen in every quarter of the globe; its colleges and theological seminaries are equipping men for every
department of human enterprise and for the pulpit. Wherever
introduced, it brings all the benefits of civilization; it pro-
motes commerce, stimulates thought, establishes schools, rears
colleges, founds hospitals, encourages art and science, erects
printing presses, issues newspapers, digs canals, tunnels mountains, extends railroads, sets up free government, settles colonies, raises cities, reclaims uncultivated lands, builds churches,
keeps the Lord's day, suppresses lawlessness, and preaches
with untiring energy the blessings of liberty and civilization
to the uttermost parts of the world.

Is Protestantism declining?

But why this world-extended interest in Martin Luther's
birthday just at this time?

Because the world has learned that Protestantism alone
fosters human liberty, and secures the rights of conscience
and private judgment.

However men may differ as to the form of government—imperial, monarchial or republican—they know well enough that
Protestanism alone will perpetuate the blessings of civilization,
maintain the authority of established government and promote
the happiness of the people. Protestants will not submit to

the domination of one man, spiritual or secular, whose single word is their law, and who prescribes to them a way to heaven upon pain of damnation—a way not found in the bible and upon which we are not allowed to judge for ourselves.

It was thought proper then to recall to Protestants the memory of the mighty man whose words were thunderbolts, and through whose agency under God the enslaved nations were disenthralled. Luther is more to Protestants than a religious Reformer. He achieved the conquest over the slavery of human thought; he freed the human conscience from riveted shackles; he is the restorer of education; he is the founder of our public schools; he is the author of national culture; he gave the first impulse to every quality that contributes to the earthly welfare of mankind. Such a man's birthday is well worth celebrating.

The only other reason I shall now give for this celebration at this time is to fire the Protestant heart against the aggressions of her enemies. Her enemies are numerous, formidable and bold.

Rationalism, materialism, with their several coadjutors, and Romanism are her worst enemies.

I speak now of systems and not of men. I accede to men the right of thinking as they please; but I claim the right of fully expressing my opinion about their thoughts. This is a Protestant privilege, and woe be to the man or church that dares to deprive us of it.

When I speak of our enemies, I mean everything that opposes the progress and nature of Protestantism, whether it be in the form of *materialism*, which would dethrone our God, or of *rationalism*, which depreciates revelation, or of *infidelity*, which rejects our bible, our Lord's Day, and would obliterate all the hallowed memories of our religious homes and Christian training, and would dissuade pious mothers from teaching their children to say, Our Father who art in heaven, or Now I lay me down to sleep; or of that politico-religious system which would abolish our public schools ; prevent the bible from being read in them ; which will not recognize our Republican Government because not sanctioned by their own foreign potentate; which never participates in the celebration of any Thanksgiving Day, or any other National holiday, because the day has been set apart by a Republican Government, whose authority it does not recognize; which denies salvation to all who do not blindly submit to its own spiritual domination ; which condemns Luther and all who with him reject its dogmas to perdition ; which aims at universal sovereignty over the minds and consciences of men, although their own leader in Rome has lost his own temporal power, and which, as the New York *Evening Post* has properly said, " has failed to prevent the immense schism known as Protestantism, and to get even a tithe of her male members to pay any attention to her ordinances ; " and this is the system which would force us all to acknowledge her rule, and dooms us all to hell because we do not.

It was thought proper that the Protestant world should hold a jubilee festival to remind us of what the man of the sixteenth century brought us, for as a popular writer of the present day says, (Harper's Monthly, Nov., 1883, p. 958,) " In the truest sense Luther is the father of modern civilization. He emancipated the human mind from ecclesiastical slavery. He proclaimed that freedom of thought without which it is easy to see that, despite the great modern inventions, the spirit of the dark ages must have been indefinitely prolonged, and the course of modern civilization must have been essentially different. It was the spiritual freedom which Luther asserted that

produced political freedom and the freedom of the press.   *   *
Indeed among human benefactors there are few greater names
than Martin Luther."

O that the soul of Luther
　Were on the earth again,
The mighty soul whose mightier faith
　Burst ancient error's chain,
And flashed the rays of God's own word
　Through superstition's night,
Till the church of God that sleeping lay,
　Awoke in Christ's own light.

The Statue,

which had been veiled with the American flag, is now unveiled,
amid bursts of applause, whilst Luther's "*Ein Feste Burg*," by
the U. S. Marine Band, gives a fitting finale.

* Unveil the hero, let him stand
With us, as in the Father land,
　A way mark in the march of Time;
Unveil him whose own hand unveiled
The modern world and Hell assailed
　With faith and courage all sublime.

Columbia hails Germania's son
As father of her Washington—
　Nor were the son without the sire;—
The freedom born of Luther's thought
Was here to forms of justice wrought
　In war's intensest furnace fire.

With Bible 'neath thy clenched hand
Upon thy granite pillar stand
　Within our nation's capital,
And whilst Potomac's silvery wave
Shall wash Mount Vernon's honored grave
　Thy name and fame shall never fall.

* Dr. Joseph Swartz's Poem.

Artistically this colossal bronze of the great Reformer is un-surpassed, whilst in inspiration it is unequaled. It stands a thing of beauty and an abiding protest against all forms of oppression, pleading, with the earnestness of four centuries, for the emancipation of conscience and of the universal man, from the despotisms which still retard the coming kingdom of the Prince of Peace.